PRAISE F
TENSION : *RUPTURE*

M000116923

"Tension : *Rupture* is a brilliant shapeshifting book that repurposes the ekphrasis as a mode of enquiry. Cutter Streeby's engagement with Michael Haight's ephemeral works, *Alcoholic Crepuscules*, offers us vivid painterly poems often laced with the surreal. There's an alchemy of sorts, a reaching into and melding into Haight's destabilizing work. Both artists operate in a zone of intensity that offers a reader different levels of immersion and experience." —MONA ARSHI

"Isolated from my friends due to the global pandemic, I'm ravenous for good conversations. Tension : *Rupture* arrived just in time. The conversation between Michael Haight and Cutter Streeby is enthralling, bright with human excess and intimacies. Streeby's poems trouble into speech the tender and volatile flesh in Haight's art, and the color in Haight's art is lyrical, transcendent. Each painting, each poem filled 'my living room with burning stars.'" —EDUARDO CORRAL

"In Tension : *Rupture*, Cutter Streeby navigates desire and poesis with language as a taut and slippery lifeline in poems complemented and complicated by Michael Haight's hallucinatory vignettes veering from bacchanal to disaster and back again. Though tonally elegiac, Streeby's poems trouble easy divisions between past and present, asking what memories still keep making us in their wakes and our awakenings. Streeby traverses time and tongues, eschewing a monolithic origin story and crafting a dazzling mosaic of originary moments instead." —DORA MALECH

"Ekphrasis has many faces. Re-enactments in one medium of a work in another can grow tedious. The true process involves touching base, understanding that base, then dancing down a course beginning in that understanding. That is the course followed by the collaboration between artist Michael Haight and poet Cutter Streeby. Here the artist's mostly water color suggestions of flesh and circumstance taken from a series titled *Alcoholic Crepuscules* prompt poems, prose, and adventures across various fields, essentially thematic but rushing off into associated imagery. It makes for an exciting set of collisions as much as collaborations. There are doors constantly opening onto potentially fierce landscapes the reader senses before being propelled onward." —GEORGE SZIRTES

"In the beautiful collaboration Tension : *Rupture* the bright architectures of bodies are ablaze on both canvas and page. Haight's vibrant colors complement the energy of Streeby's lines, and the union confronts the rending of intimacy with a rendering of it. Here among the heliotropes and blood halos, 'language is a conspiracy between two people.' Figure and syllabary create a dialogue across this book, giving a name to each feeling and a voice to every fire." —TRACI BRIMHALL

TENSION : RUPTURE

TUPELO PRESS
2021

TENSION : RUPTURE

POEMS BY **CUTTER STREEBY**

PAINTINGS BY **MICHAEL HAIGHT**

Tension: *Rupture*

ISBN 978-1-946482-58-7 (pb)
ISBN 978-1-946482-66-2 (hb)

Design by adam b. bohannon
Cover image by Michael Haight
Copyright © 2021. Used with permission of the artist.

First paperback edition: November 2021
Library of Congress Catalog-in-Publication data available upon request.

Tupelo Press
P.O. Box 1767
North Adams, Massachusetts 01247
(413) 664-9611 / Fax: (413) 664-9711
editor@tupelopress.org / www.tupelopress.org

Tupelo Press is an award-winning independent literary press that publishes fine fiction, nonfiction, and poetry in books that are a joy to hold as well as read. Tupelo Press is a registered 501(c)(3) nonprofit organization, and we rely on public support to carry out our mission of publishing extraordinary work that may be outside the realm of the large commercial publishers. Financial donations are welcome and are tax deductible.

C O N T E N T S

Introduction   ix

P A I N T I N G S

Alcoholic Crepuscule #5   4
(Cambridge Ave.)

Alcoholic Crepuscule #6   8
(Bailey's House)

Alcoholic Crepuscule #7   12
(Old English 800)

Alcoholic Crepuscule #8   14, 53
(Insomniacs PC Lounge)

Alcoholic Crepuscule #9   15
(Hangover Junction)

Alcoholic Crepuscule #10   18
(UC Riverside Botanical Gardens)

Alcoholic Crepuscule #11   22
(The House on the Hill)

Alcoholic Crepuscule #12   27
(Chau's House)

Alcoholic Crepuscule #13   28
(Brandon's Ranch)

AlcoholicCrepuscule #14   32
(Leah's House)

Alcoholic Crepuscule #15   36
(Guri City)

Alcoholic Crepuscule #16   40
(Todd's House)

Alcoholic Crepuscule #17   43
(Club Infiniti)

Alcoholic Crepuscule #18   46
(Pledge Class Scavenger Hunt)

Alcoholic Crepuscule #19   47, 54, 56
(Trojan Ct.)

POEMS

Framework : A Vessel   3

The Pickup Line   7

Ela   10

Detail : Garnet   11

~~Letter from a New City to an Old Friend~~   13

Concerning the Fox   16

Detail : Liber Monstrorum   17

Florilegium : Voynich Manuscript   21

Salamanders   24

Adam & Adam   26

Ben's Ranch : A Fence of Clouds   31

Ansia : Reach   33

Detail : λέγω   34

White Elephants   37

Sand Castles   39

Portrait of the Psyche : Mycology   41

Tonic Key : A Rose   45

One   48

Detail : Heliotrope   50

Framework : i   52

Self-Portrait through the Eyes of a Photographer   55

Afterword by Jane Ursula Harris   59

Notes   61

INTRODUCTION

Whether we admit it or not, we're always in dialogue with what has come before and what will follow. The self is never autonomous but exists within and against a nexus of formative relationships that are never static, but always evolving.* We live the present simultaneously through our histories and our projected futures; more precisely, we live at the intersection of those two moments. For poets, for creative people in general who live in a perpetual state of creation, we move from day to day, from project to project, amassing artifacts of who we are that become who we used to be. A painting from last year, a picture we took a decade ago—like a chain of islands—these let us look back and quite literally plot the changes of our internal geography over time. "Things are different now." That's almost always how it goes. If we're honest, if we're open to growth, we should always actively interrogate our interior landscapes, enter into dialogue with the private terrain of our habits of mind and with our subjective realities. Who we were is not who we have to be tomorrow. As creatives, as self-aware humans, we should always seek to transcend ourselves with the next creative act; and the best way to find our edges is to open a dialogue with ourselves and the outside world.

Growth comes from dialogue, from points of contact between unmerged, independent voices where our self-perceived identities can be challenged by opposing views. If we enter into genuine dialogue, we will be brought face-to-face with the our edges of our worlds. We will find the places where things just don't add up and having discovered these unstable territories, we can choose to shore up or raze the underlying architecture of "I," and make new

* Deborah J. Haynes, "Bakhtin and the Visual Arts," in Paul Smith and Carolyn Wilde, eds., *A Companion to Art Theory* (Oxford, MA: Blackwell, 2002), 292–302.

choices in the next set of creative pieces. The project before you is just that—two artists figuring out how to combine their different aesthetic languages into a single, comprehensive panorama that serves the reader. There are paths in Tension : *Rupture* that lead nowhere, there are leaps of faith here that carry us beyond ourselves, and there is also here the high ground at the intersection of two languages.

This project started simply: at the start of the pandemic, I reached out to my friend Michael Haight and asked if he'd be interested in responding to a selection of my poems by painting his reactions. We had attended college together and as I came to find out over the course of our work, he had battled with addiction during that time, the same as I. I sent him my unpublished manuscript and asked him to find some poems to which he felt a connection and to move them across into his medium of images. Seems simple, right? "Here's my working collection of poems, it hasn't been published and is still 'unformed' and open to changes, so just pick some out and paint your interpretations." But like any truly intimate dialogue where the speakers have different histories and futures, where the voices are independent, this project evolved into the present with each exchange.

In my collection, there is a series of poems called "Frameworks" that act as narrative keys; Haight picked these and proposed a response series called "Alcoholic Crepuscules" that explored his battle with alcoholism. He "translated" his experienced narrative from my poems into his medium, into a language of watercolor, tempera, and gouache. When I got these images back, the paintings themselves held something similar to my own narrative—they were a documentation, a recreation of Haight during his time in the grips of addiction. The paintings were fluid, the objects unformed and dissolving; the memories were a decade old and seemed foreign, like something seen in another life. The color palette is twilight or sunrise; blue and yellow figure prominently in all of his scenes. The project could have ended there, my narrative "Frameworks" a monologue illustrated by his own I paintings. However, I saw in the borderlands between our works an opportunity to push forward into an even more honest, legitimate dialogue. It was the tension I felt in reading his paintings that persuaded me to go further than simple ekphrasis.

We were different. My addiction was different. My friends that had OD'd and died were not his friends. The bedrock of my identity was different, so I determined to allow Haight's visual works to hold the narrative line and I selected or wrote new poems that I felt offered a more individuated rendering, poems that set me apart from his narration. After I sent these new poems back to Haight, he selected "details" from his paintings, a way visual artists say, "This part is the most important to me"—I responded by writing my own "Details" and adding them to the conversation. Agency of creation, the "speaking roles" in this project, switched hands often during the process and the result is a layered amalgamation of interpretations and a reverberation of meanings between our respective mediums. I open with a poem; he closes with a painting. At each exchange, there is an intersection, a tension, a rupture between our languages and our memories, our own stylized selves expressed through our languages that results in new islands, new continents of awareness.

TENSION : RUPTURE

Framework : A Vessel
Notes on a Grecian Urn

We should say how it starts, shouldn't we? Wet clay and water, finger-formed—should say it's spun, formed from a controlled force, built over a locus.

There's control there, pressure and something bigger bearing down on something more malleable, responsive. But the pair in this image, shaper and the shaped, learn both ways . . . one teaching control, one teaching release, and who's to say which way that knowledge flows : up or down.

When you reach a certain point everything becomes that way : spinning clay, formed in an instant of perception, reassessed, adjusted.

I see myself now, years later, differently than before, but I know the truth of it like this : what it is, is spinning, what I *am* is responding to pressures from the outside in, and from the inside out, equally.

The Pickup Line

you tell me you *waited on a god today* : brought him

carpaccio with parmesan and tea : called him sting : or

springsteen : i'm not surprised : you tell me the floor was

glass over tar pits in la brea and how if i come down

i'll show you the exposed bones and flesh and hide : i'm

not surprised : you'd show me where he sat at the bar :

how he said : *it's only the starting that's hard for me*

darling : fine then i'll come down and you show me :

granada : pomegranate seed : : tell me something :

anything : tell me i'm a fool in the glory of your animal and

that i was stripped and seen : tell me i'm an entire fool

continent of people with a ferris wheel over the city and a

tower and miles and miles of river : tell me you think i'm

fragrant at the bottom of the vessel like balsam : tell me

how you ran your finger flat around his bowl when he left

: *put it in your mouth* : sucked it clean

Ela

que se levanta de la tierra : what rises from the earth : *y se hace humana* : becomes human : sunlight falls and we don't move with it : we move in it : *can you feel the difference* : if we just shift our mental position : can we invest an object with a deeper reverence : *say i play the host and cook you dinner tonight* : *would that be alright* : sure : flesh of my flesh : : a new reference : it's the biology of belief and it's all the worlds we carry with us that produce the movement we see : how water wheat yeast and salt become sacred and save a people : eucharistic : this theater is poetry itself that rises from the earth and becomes human : *fines dei* : *realgar* : red tint : *a la caída de la tarde* : a thunderhead at the fall of the day : *y al hacerse habla* : and when it moves it speaks : *grita* : it grumbles : *llora y se despera* : it cries and becomes desperate : : it's eleven o'clock and the sun is set and i'm still amazed at how ink blots on a page become butterflies : how rain drops on the pavement become black birds or planes or the crow tattooed on your chest : *thunderstorms turn me on so badly* : how the streetlight reflecting on the water : once painted : becomes the impression of a couple : *i wish the storm lasts until the night* : *is my english right* : : yes : i'm looking for a word that tastes like your red : *sandarac* : *vespertino* : the music of red : heat from the sun dripping into the river breaks the water into smaller pieces that rise up on the wind : *que se levanta* : and this theatre that rises : *del agua y se hace rubicundo* : our garnet blades coalescing in the pregnant clouds : their bellies full of virgin birds whose skin is stained scarlet with the things they eat : our rain : i'm looking for a word that means that band of light right above the cathedral where for one instant the water is a net of blood hung over our city : that's where i'm sketching this picture of us : before it falls : through and turns back into water : i'm looking for a word that runs like your red : pure grapes and alcoholic : *deslumbrar* : blinding light : *centellear* : i need a word : that bites like your tannins on my tongue

Detail : Garnet

Garnet blades coalesce in pregnant clouds.
Clouds, their bellies full of virgin birds;

    The cloud skin of your belly taut, full.
    How can water, wheat and yeast save a people?

Water, wheat, and yeast can save a people—how
Is a word that means *change* or *transform*;

    Change meaning, transform the word for
    A halo of rain around the cathedral's crown:

Blood haloes from the cathedral's crown—
That's one way to say that change is holy.

~~Letter from a New City to an Old Friend~~ [SEAside Gra-
-i.m. ~~Ronny Burhop 1987-2010~~   Steve Cafagna 1986 – 2019
ffiti]

[adjust   Even the white noise here is different—
   trACKing]   there's no boulevard, no blue ~~and breathing~~
                 ocean. The streets—quieter now, winding
                 through ~~rain, hidden~~ parks and open markets—
                                                      [chriiiiiiing]
                 are cobbled, and twist off into alleys
                 less sinister than ours. There's ~~history~~ [REprise]
                 ~~in the~~ street names, true—but ~~the mystery~~,
                 the footsteps' muffled click, the concrete ~~sea~~
bRZeE

                 ~~rolling below my window~~ is tame,
                 bloodless . . .
                         [BRiX '98]
                 We fell off ~~the world~~ for years in LA.   [So
                 I can only remember the haze now,   eAcH   corP.
                 ~~how our vista was never really clear~~   oWn

                 of smog, or planes, or neon-bellied clouds.   a sOul?]
                 I split. Left you standing with a pocket
[My grambag   full of lock-
                    of   less keys, a few bucks, two lighters and I
tRixY   drove ~~the forty miles~~ back home. Years later,
rEds]   I'm hoping, perhaps we can just look back,
tuchhhh—   —MIDAZ
                 recall it before the cards were flipped—
                 ~~our own Cassidy and Sundance era~~?   (EPIX
                                       x
                 I turned my back on California,   X)
                 on ~~those two-for-one, from out the Honda~~
[Malverde]   ~~hustlers, the sunburned homeless~~, los santos . . .
                 And I have thought about nothing else, since.
                 I heard ~~about your dazzling surrender~~.
[oUr buRnT-   Guess I should ask ~~'from whose bourn' and all that~~,
                 but I can't fucking see how it matters.
                                                    oUt   SCAPE]

                         Anyways, it's probably December
                 right now in your coastal town, every crow   * JauREZ—
                 crowding the power lines, jostling. Each one   Bosnia
                 vacant, thinking only of ~~its single~~
                 ~~green walnut~~, the distance to the pavement.   del SUR*
                 Damn— it's been over
'grAFT'   ~~NoV16, 2009~~ 6.16.2019   a ~~ten~~ years now

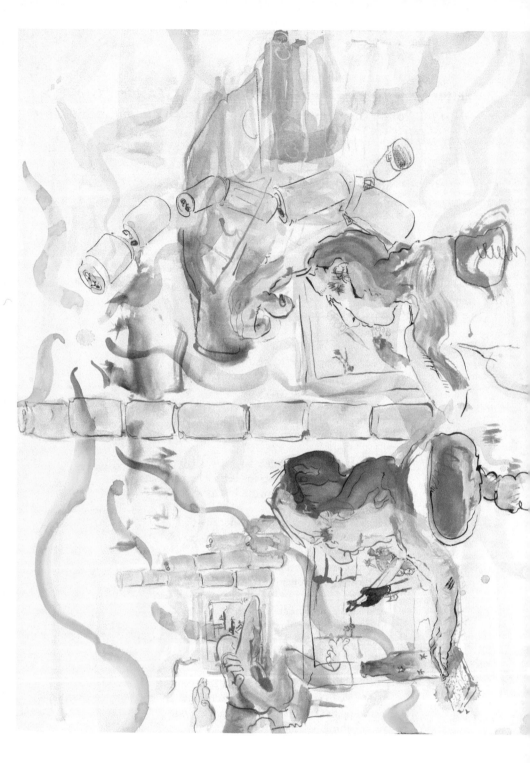

Concerning the Fox
Liber Monstrorum

the way you touch me has changed since the beginning : tell me how : *i couldn't even explain it in spanish* : in english : : it's different : : *you touch me different* : maybe you feel different : *maybe* : maybe there's two sides to this : a purple grade of red : a continuum : or maybe it's the start of something : *or an end* : : *write it down then go ahead* : i am : *i can see the images in your brain* : *tu mente se vuelve transparente* : it's like you're becoming transparent and you're taking all of my words and editing them into the other things you steal : that's true : i am : : *ladrón de manzanas* : *you came out as a whirlwind to scatter me* : you're doing the same : *fingir* : the fox : *he's the same here and people chase him away* : *oscurecer* : but being hungry he finds him a new way which he hopes to ensnare some singing birds for his prey : supine and crossing his legs himself in a furrow he stretches : *fruncir* : *you're stealing all of my things* : i noticed it too : but i want your words : and your body : and your mind in my hands : *why is everything moving so fast and intense with you* : and lying as if he were dead : *and i'm perfectly fine with it* : scarce drawing breath until the crow : *cuervo* : or the stork : *cigüeña* : *i like the word because you have to say the u* : *that's what those marks mean* : : *marcas del sueño* : what do those marks mean : : and some other birds seeing the sleeping fox now thinking a corpse they'll find : they light on the fox hoping him food : *you don't know how cautious and distant i usually am with humans that try to get this close* : and quickly the fox rises up : and suddenly seizes one flying : : *i see what you're doing* : do you : *and it's funny to me* : *you think you're the fox* : but whose flesh he eats becomes him : *but i'm the one on my back in this bed* : transfixed : *and you're eating me* and i'm transfigured like truth by words : *creos* in greek is *caro* in latin is *flesh* in english and *you* in spanish at the table last night : *morcilla* : *this is not my blood* : *it's for you* : : *i like mine with rice and piñones* : and my whole world wants one sharp stone : *crux interpretum* : that you may strip off my skin so we can be at once : *simuli* or by the composition of our bodies derived : *dissimulare* : to pretend : that he does not know that which he knows : or not to be that which he is : : *you need a break pibón* : *just come lay down here and show me those eyes*

Detail : Liber Monstrorum

You've asked about the secret arrangement,
That I record the creatures most fearful to men.

> To record the creatures most fearful to men,
> Realize first that fear is projected.

Projected fear, realized, is first
Founded inside the man by what he doesn't know.

> What you don't know about this man: he's founded
> Mostly in the alcoholic breath of women.

The alcoholic breath of a woman is mostly
Mother to him, mostly his whole childhood.

> Mostly alcohol mothered him his whole childhood:
> *Kneel down here, look up; now show me those eyes.*

I'm still down there, looking up, showing my eyes
In a secret arrangement I couldn't ask about.

Florilegium : Voynich Manuscript

i'll start with what i was given : : organic threads and purple flowers
tyrian : serrated bulbs and a woman with her arms open pushed
into roots bisected : filling with water : : in reality : *the division of
the sexes is the most elegant metaphor of the human being* : and the
psyche : a

manuscript indecipherable and she is my joint and anatomy : her
text so smoothly written the ductus is fluid and does not appear
enciphered : and we can never know who we will be : excepting
what we choose today : and we can never know who we will be : *i
wonder if it'll be*

different tomorrow : or what evil may be necessary to produce the
good : *i should* : or union : *do something* : : opposites from opposites :
a tower : a black creek : not really black but the environment around
it black : : *transference* : to the trees : the sky : : maybe it was gray

: maybe i was wrong : : and we say to the woman within us : *raca*
and condemn and rage against ourselves : and it's in this moment
of our disarray : in that vertigo before you wake up : when you come
to understand that you won't ever wake up : and that vertigo : *your
feet off the bed and*

the sun again through the window : that vertigo is just living : and it's
this moment that i realize i'm just settling into my own

body : coming to fill my fingers to the ends

Salamanders

one flame in july : the progression : *viral* : : images of firefighters
flashover the screen : pilots scatter retardant : red clouds bursting
from the bellies of planes : : pieces of the inferno go dark : briefly
: but things are opened in flames : *but things are opened in flames* :
seed pods : the trunks of trees : meadows : *meadows* : : when the
fires are

bright the clouds at night are a canvas for the shadow play of moths
: planes between clouds and flames : it's this negative space that
could always be our own story : told in hotspots and wings : : for
most people it's an analgesic : the neighbor's short-sell : our celeb-
rity diets : who got the

call-up to the majors : conversations of hospice : *they do long-term
sickness now : not just the dying* : aurora colorado : minneapolis min-
nesota : to each his own shadows play on the light inside flames :
can you see : it's a holy dissolution that's why it's so enthralling : :
maybe

fire is summer's summer : a natural hunger : maybe my country
feeds on the season's need for self-immolation : maybe skyscrapers
are conduits : derricks over the desire for flame and drawn up : past
asphalt and sewers : it pours

out : to settle like ash : like blue-veined bats that grow as they de-
scend : then fan their wings and change their faces and walk like
humans on the street : : what's true : *what's*

true : whether the devastation wrought is natural or induced : :
doesn't really matter

Adam & Adam

For Jorge Sarabia

so early here : how strange *: a skeleton* and from the blank rain of me

a street : a silver sign : and it seemed his legs without knees un-

: quivered below me : so soon : and for you how quickly forgettable
this : : as a bird i come

against you in the evening : and whistling my green song : plant in
your mouth : a forest :

: *you come to me in the evening* and your roost : an amber eye : your
roost : a constellation holding true

: north : and the sun and red wine and us un- : covered : and our
forest : *pre-* : fire : prefigured : pre- :

bronze music : and your face unsanctioned in the mirror : and me :
lapis : a blue feather : *wind* : dust in the window's corner : our tem-
pest temporary and flailing : :

and holding out your long hand you come again : a blue wind shaking
the trees and our clock undone and the hour uncoupled to springs
and light : below me the water

in the gutter silvers : slivers : the body of my building leaking peo-
ple clothed in morning and dew and your song unwavered : still up
: muscle-roped :

still *living* : legged like a man : sheets : there was : *this* : always this
: slow- : down :

        drift you say : you : say : and you're

        gone again : *fugaz* : a brief burning :

atmospheric and ozone :

fugaz : the way you filled our living room with burning stars

26

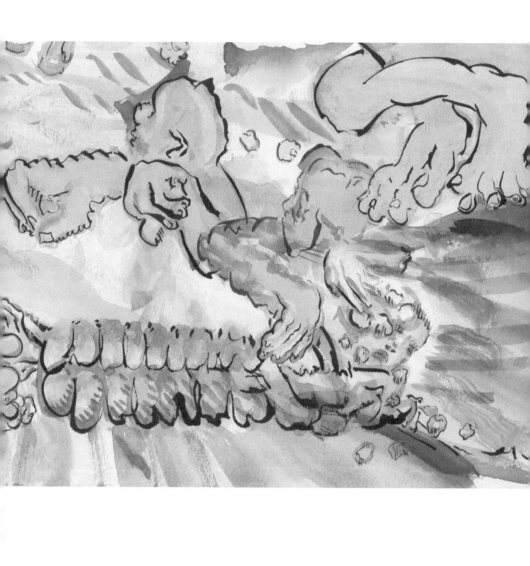

Ben's Ranch : A Fence of Clouds

i'm opening with this : a man visible from his thick thighs up : breaking through snow hip high and the moon a huge mirror strapped to his back and there's a song i can't hear playing in his mind : and that music is his alone :

as yours is : : and mine : : there are events that happen rarely : *rara avis in terres* : a rare thing that shapes the melody or the horizon inside the moon-man's mind : we call it *love* or *pandemic* or once when i was in college

there was a kid who'd never seen the snow and i took him to a mountain there and found it : i remember him getting out of the car to touch it and he moved so slowly like he was in a movie : and i was surprised when he started to cry : how his tears became geometry : *we don't have this in my country* : freezing out from the corners of his eyes : *and i came here to learn it* : we were young then but still male : still : *marble* : and the word i need comes from

architecture and describes the raised space between the channels carved in a triglyph : *femur* : young then still tied to muscle and limb and founded on the brittle strength of bones : *we were both rapt though weren't we* : we were : wrapped in tendon and tears and even writing that i feel too maudlin : *we can't have this in my country* : but i watched him bend to touch the snow : *femoral* : *it's the largest bone in the body and the hardest to break* : ephemeral : and his thighs were roped and too big and when he bent it opened a dark sea between the waist

of his jeans and the unstained anatomy of his lower back and we build what we will under that : *what are you doing* : *we should leave here together and get food* : whether we admit it or not : *weather* : : the world spins

and it snows : the world spins and it's spring : *change* : and the song changes too but slowly and looking back now i see his hand forming an ampoule for storing liquid : medicine : a glass carafe and i see our clear medium tinged with white and frozen clouds grown into a great nation of sky

Ansia : Reach

your body on the bed as a glyph : λέγω : : a darkness above intellect : cataphatic : and i can't enter into that darkness without darkness without you : : *mi cuerpo no escucha ya ni a tus manos* : *my body can't hear your hands* : and your eyes

read me like the language of fans : moving and archaic : but i'm writing past names now and into the over-them : using your body on the bed as a glyph : λέγω : *to say* : a name made invisible by a name : *lego* : *llegas por fin* : pointing the way to a place without end : *primero* :

con los dedos : first with fingers : *que acarician levemente* : light touch on soft lip scarred : and entering here we shall find not sound as such : *warm tunnel* : the oracles say : but an utter absence of conception : : *mucho más rocío empapándolo todo* : *the dew on the ground of me is pooling again* :

the dew on the ground of me is pooling again : and i need the same thing from you : eyes closed : our prayer : : your mind purred white noise and me : blank-space : between your body and mine so the soul : not-soul : the watcher inside

can stand free from the noise of our matter : *apenas rozando* : : and it comes with a choking and stretching sound from its latin roots : gendered words and we are twined and twisted but of nothing and in nothing and signifying nothing except exchange and

approach at first slowly the oracles say : *apenas rozando* : what is : : is pre-word and naming it makes invisible your form in me as darkness is made invisible by light : : at the point of absorption : you are and are not : : and we feel without feeling toward an earth without form where our bodies are a vehicle of silence : *después* :

volverás camino arriba : *your mouth coming up to meet mine* : you are the feeling i have before i find the words : not the words : a name made invisible by a name : *para que yo pueda probarme en tu boca* : : you are my way into that place undefined : redefined without sound by our tongues : *y la carne dentro de la carne* : the flesh inside the flesh : : the place where we are the word inside the god

Detail : λέγω

To say is the crux because everything's there.
What is, is pre-word and to say

It's pre-word means *impossible to say.* But if I could get close to
sketching,

Close to sketching . . . if I could—
To say *I loved you then* is worthless.

To give a reason is worth less than saying love—
Reason grows from the root of *legos,*

And if we can't *say* a thing, logos can't be there:
X   XXxxxy   x   XXX   XX   xx x

xxxxY   X   xxxxxxxx Y y   x
Yyyyyyyyyyy   y   xxx X   xxx   y

Y   y yyyyy yyyyyyyyyyy yyy y
So breath's form's the crux then? Everything's there.

White Elephants

they degrade in retelling : *memory's plastic and whatever's in the environment around you can rewrite the original* : : let me use this written language : *what do we do* : let me use these half-formed symbols for signs in a semblance of order : *please don't* : then let me use one without words : my hand on your hand : : *we can't go back* : cerebellum : *antebellum* : how you played the piano at your dad's : but not in front of me : how my sons offered themselves to you for a hug : : to go further back's too hard in my own language : it feels like : : like : let me use yours : *la forma en que tu boca* : like it's always prettier : *en la mía se sintió lo cementa* : it doesn't matter really : this retelling : this act won't cement it because memory's plastic and the very act of remembering can change it : will change it : *el lugar donde pasó importa* : place matters though in the making of memories : spatial orientation : *place the pieces you wish to remember in places you know well where to walk* : that's how you memorize things : simonides : : you on a street in sevilla back flat on a flatiron building : *a painting that talks* : arms outstretched in a cross : : two paths on either side cobbled together in the same orange light : or was it california : twin visions in an autumn fog : or helena : a trine : : how many times have i been here : pink myrtle shedding leaves like hands : your hand on the test in the breast pocket of a blue scrub top : *we have to talk* : just stop : i can't : : *the strength of emotion makes the memory last* : i'll say it clearly then if i can : i remember being here before : i remember feeling the tree of my soul grafted to the flesh of another : *in* : osculate : pine sap or collar bone : *cicatrices* or rose : i remember the tearing sound : *el avión llega en media hora* : what did she say : *the plane comes in half an hour* : that's what i remember most : the tearing sound like train brakes in London : i remember pain in the shape of your hand curled on the half of your face i could see in the night : but my memory's becoming transparent : *que mi memoria se vuelve transparente* : *it's just that i've lost so much already* : i don't know what to do : *que mis palabras tambien*

Sand Castles

let's see what i find here looking for nothing : waves : shells in the sand : a new beach and crowds of people : our boys lost in a rhythm they don't understand : instinct maybe : : *do you think the ladies saw me dad* : push and pull : genetic : our letters in a bottle : what will i find looking for nothing : : below the jewel-colored clouds : i'm still here at the joint of soul and body : holding : running my pen over the seams of me : : scar tissue mostly : mountains : : myself writing you again : *it's just another city* : *less busy than ours* : more violent : : the jewel-colored tides are the same though : *pulled by the moon* : storms are the same here too : twisted by the spin of the earth : my partner now : *i'm trying to settle into this relationship* : *i've stopped talking to other people* : heat from the sun heating the clouds : *you'll have to trust me* : spinning the storms : billions of years and the diamond of my momentum the same : *how can i trust you* : it comes in : goes out : the history of man where fear is the living country between us : : *how could you lie again* : : let's see what i find when looking for nothing : our two boys : four and six : chasing sea foam back below the waterline : running from the tide : *i wanted a baby too* : covered in sand : : and what they are given is earth : *las locuras de sus padres* : a body : and they shall inherit our madness : *but i wanted it to be with you* : : what do i find here *my abortion's scheduled for the twenty-fourth* : this beach is our palace : and its pattern : : our glory

Portrait of the Psyche : Mycology

you can identify mushrooms by the presence of their juices on breaking :
bright smell or earthen : or whether or not they exhibit a bruising : a
light coral gone blue where her thumbnail

pressed the flesh : that's how you know which ones change your
mind : *celeste* : or maybe it goes amber and ash : heather : or scarlet
and on and on and each one has its season : its habit

and its shade of colors : the vivid blue gills on an indigo when you
split the veil : virile : : before that : founded in a deep mass of webs :
ebony : *hyphae* : just a hint of warmth in the wetness : call it

mycelium : my ceiling : my sky : :

it's in the dark warmth the overlay becomes apparent : it ruptures
and becomes lips or caps or eyes : : and if a life takes say : *natural
birth :* say everything goes to plan : then these earlier stages become
remnants in the new body : *recombination* : old memories in new
bodies : the skirt on an amanita : *aman* : the sea : : or you'll find it like

collars on a lepiota : *felina* : : a cellular form : the cat you kept on our
balcony in france named lefty from the word lepis meaning *scale* :
and that's how we name them isn't it : *sui generis* : microscopic pat-
terns and floral : or by their scents and warnings and fear : *don't*

eat those and *do try these* and *never have i ever* and most of us go tasting
only what we're given : *bright lights* and *fluorescent* : scared to try the
other colors and blindly trusting what other people term forbidden :
hand clasped

to something someone else has granted : *this is the way :* we go tasting
nothing : *the only way : pray like this :* not knowing how flesh yields

beneath teeth : how memory : *the flesh of our world :* unravels : how
after ingestion liquids are split

and dissolve : a hidden millennia poured into mine

Tonic Key : A Rose

Reality is infinitely shifting and tangled together and we cast our mortal, static selves over the starscape of space and time, and expect that outside world to fall into human lines. And then we get upset when pieces move without consent. And it's worse than that. We can't see what we don't know, and I mean that literally. We are blind to it.

Watch this. Say you grew up in New York City with traffic and the endless murmur of the people and subways and bus routes and you've never been fishing in a mountain stream in your life.

Imagine you've never been fishing in your whole life. When you stand in front of the water here in Montana, you know nothing of the way water bends around a rock and that fish sit in the pockets. You will see the style of water running left to right and see the blank face of a cliff with sparrows, the water a broken mirror reflecting the sky and your own face. You'll feel the cold on your feet when you step in; that's it.

Ten thousand hours. You have to learn to read the water for the fish in here to be more than luck or prayer; to be real. The objects we experience in our world call us based on our perceptual arc, based on the worlds we carry with us.

I limit the infinity of the world by the variable of what calls to me from it. Language is a good example.

Language is a conspiracy between two people, and it's always only two, necessarily: the speaker and the hearer, no matter the scale; the words hit your ear only, process in your mind only. Your space, your time.

To me the word *rose* on the page occupies a different position in my world than yours, but in the net of our language, *rose* can be a rough approximation for a physical or metaphysical object. I can never know what *rose* is to you, exactly. And that's amazing.

Say I write it down and let it go on the stream above, *rose*—it's one thing to me, but can be a million different things to you, always.

It can be a million different things, always.

One

the splayed ones naked on this bed : call one hosanna : call one heliotrope : one a genre of sun : : call one two things : flower and stone : call one faceless : : call one reap : call one *burn* in this image : watch the forest of a cheek become another texture for a tongue : watch one anoint the other : *hoc est corpus meum* : : : now follow one here : watch one flay the top layer of skin : *does one have dreams* : watch one voiceless : : watch one expose muscles that twitch : white tendon and blood : watch word : safe word : watch one open : watch one tremble : watch one tell one one's brother's name is cole : how one's boyfriend who was twenty-two carved a name into one's leg : s—n : and that one was fourteen : watch one say *something like that happened to one once* : except one was six then :

watch one too twisted : write the other : watch one say to one : *kneel and make me what i am* : watch one kneel : watch one belong to one's darkness : watch one find it : watch one's delight in darkness like in the tents of kedar : watch one open for the other : : how one whispers horse names like a prayer whenever that one is scared : *haizum* : *keshi* : *cheval merlette* : the saddled horse who comes every night riderless and stands by one's bed : *one always dreams of horses* : watch one's hand tree shaped : sink into one's chest : *now one dreams them too* : watch one's body become a lambda : : look at one's face turned up in these lines : cratered by the sun of one's eyes : blacked out : watch one crumple at one's feet like paper when one's done : spent fuel : carbon fiber : watch one become a tau

scribbled on one's door : that's how one works : feels : like for like :
body for body : watch one sow : watch how one buries the ropes of
one's name in one's flesh : how one earns the anatomy and maps
it : thigh : collar bone : the hanoverian in one's throat : watch one
cavalier : watch one horse-born : : watch one flay : watch one lay the
live light of one's name over one's stomach in a wet line : : watch
one's flesh stand : watch one finger find it : watch

one open one from the navel up : watch one zip one with a tongue
: : watch one's fingers read the raised braille of one's name on one's
skin : watch one burn in this image : *candled* : watch one dripping
wax : watch one light the word inside : *gratia plena* : votive : *salve
regina* : let one burn forever : *o dulcis virgo maria* : one's street with
one's

tongue

Detail : Heliotrope

genre of   sun

two   things

flower   and stone

the forest of   [us]   of   [us]

a genre

a safe   word

carved in

delight

[we] *always dream of horses*

dream them

feet like   paper

taus

the forest of   [our]

cheek

body for   body   [we]

cavalier and   horse-born

[we]   a genre   of

live light

raised braille

[our] names
                        candled

votive

Framework : i

Let's just be blunt and get it over with—I was born before my time, not a prophet, I mean my parents are old enough to be most people's grandparents. I was alive before movement.

I can't justify the nations of my history, but I can look back and pick the paths and the revolutions that birthed me. Find the details I want to keep for me, say *that's where I started, right there.*

I can find the different textures, mark off the failures, the *not enough, not even close to enough done* points in my own past, and seen, try to change them going forward. I can't erase them, but I can find a pattern or a thread, I can liberate a light that feels right like *I wish I would have : but then again* here I am.

And no, not like the Gestalts. I don't think there's a mystical, collective unconscious, something underwriting the way our brains make a triangle from a set of random dots. We're thrown into the world running, knowing voice in the mother's belly, knowing lights before *me.*

We have to pick—to redefine . . . I have to pick the points of my change. I don't really remember how it happened, but I could tell you a story if you pressed me. The first time my dad caught me with a boy, I think he thought to fix me. I was six then.

Self-Portrait through the Eyes of a Photographer

you tell me you take your men from different angles and catch them in your frame and gather them in your drag : and looking at your wall that holds them all : i imagine you make them like fish of the sea : you see : natural : and you show me images and images and images pinned in their poses and say look : *they are beautiful here* : and the meat of this city is plenteous for me : and i ask if you've been captured before : and you show me a picture of yourself hung in the black ropes and dancing and say : *this is aerial silk* : the art of suspension : *from when i was younger in lima* : : and it is dark in our city and your studio is cold tonight and the light from my computer is blue over us and *alma inversa* you say reading my first four lines : *alma inversa* : these men are not animals *ayes* : eyes : your name for me then : but people : people i love in the moment i am with them : *te amo* : *pero te ves en mis llamas* : : you see yourself in my flames

AFTERWORD
Jane Ursula Harris

"how memory : the flesh of our world : unravels"

Michael Haight's series, *Alcoholic Crepuscules, 2017–2021*, features fluid, dissolving figures in space that map the physical and emotional terrain of youth. Rendered in watercolor, tempera, and gouache, the scenes he limns recall his coming of age in the streets of California's Inland Empire, where sunsets and drinking go hand in hand.

A fancy word for twilight, crepuscule—as Haight reminds me—can refer to sunrise as well as sunset, to the golden hour and the blue hour. Not surprisingly, yellow and blue figure prominently in his suburban landscapes, and in the houses, curbs, and yards he depicts where he and his friends drank. These places have the shape-shifting contours of daydreams and nightmares alike, and while some are based on photographs, they are like palimpsests seen through the shimmer of memory.

The figures that inhabit them have the essence of vapor too, dissolving and forming in response to their environments, and reflecting the transience of their remembering. The story they tell is one of wild abandon, an adolescent rite of passage familiar to so many, rife with the giddy pleasures of boozing it up, of garrulous insights and outsized gestures. Their hyperbolic, mythic sense of communion is paradoxically sacred and false. These drunken moments are wanly expressed throughout, tinged with the anticipation of what will almost inevitably follow: that ugly reckoning of self with self that can no longer be forestalled by a seemingly endless night. This dissolution is amplified by the wobbly beer can towers his figures build, and the cars they turn into impromptu clubs, none of which were built to last.

Alcoholic Crepuscules spans the arc of Haight's drinking years, from high school to college, when he began to contend with his alcoholic tendencies. Scenes of the quad and botanical gardens at the University of California–Riverside mix with those of the frat house where he befriended Cutter Streeby. The two shared a love of literature and drinking, and the book you hold is an homage to that love and friendship. It is a collaboration forged as well from a mutual belief in the power of the mnemonic imagination. What unfolds in the pairings of Haight's paintings with Streeby's poems is a tender, solicitous exchange; a call-and-response across time and medium that summons forth the act of self-creation.

Tension : *Rupture* opens with Streeby's poem "Framework : A Vessel (Notes on a Grecian Urn)," invoking the Romantic tradition of ekphrastic poetry by way of Keats. The ekphrastic is for Streeby both a strategy and metaphor, a means to traverse the tremulous world of Haight's *Alcoholic Crepuscules*, and illuminate it with words. Vivid descriptions of the sun, impenetrable blocks of text, annotations that visualize time, excerpts recomposed, all become manifestations of Streeby's presence in Haight-land, of what he deems in one work, "the watcher inside."

The book ends with a detail of *Alcoholic Crepuscules, #19 (Trojan House)*, a self-portrait of sorts. It depicts a cartoonish Haight naked with his cat on the gabled roof of a party house. He sits precariously perched at the tip, watching a raucous party unfold below him, disengaged and yet somehow ready to jump off. The detail image hones in on the scene below, where another lone figure stands apart from the crowd by the shadowy edge of the house. He looks contemplatively off into the distance as he grasps a glass with a red liquid to his chest. Perhaps he is Streeby, perhaps he is us.

In the poem "One," which accompanies the full work, the reader is compelled through lush evocative images to watch and watch again: "watch one too twisted : write the other" . . . "watch one's delight in darkness like in the tents of kedar" . . . "watch one light the word inside." That last line might be the perfect guide to navigating this book, encouraging each of us to reclaim from the landscapes of our own past those word-worlds within that will help us to carry on, and create ourselves anew.

NOTES : IN DIALOGUE

"FRAMEWORK : A VESSEL"

"The idea of heteroglossia comes as close as possible to conceptualizing a locus where the great centripetal and centrifugal forces that shape discourse can meaningfully come together."

>   Michael Holquist, *Dialogism: Bakhtin and His World*
>   (Routledge, 2002).

"THE PICKUP LINE"

Italicized portions are from a conversation I had with Bonnie Hernandez about a conversation that may have occurred in La Brea at some point.

"O felix conditor terrae, nive albior, suavitate dulcior, f[r]agrans in fundo vasis instar balsami." (O blest creator of the earth, whiter than snow, sweeter than sweetness, fragrant at the bottom of the vessel like balsam.)—Nicholas Melchior of Hermannstadt. Translated by Carl G. Jung

>   Carl G. Jung, *Collected Works*, Vol. 12, *Psychology and Alchemy*
>   (Pantheon Books, 1953).

"ELA"

Some of the Spanish in "Ela" is pulled from the following quote by Federico García Lorca:

>   "El teatro es la poesía que se levanta del libro y se hace humana. Y al hacerse, habla y grita, llora y se desespera. El teatro necesita que los personajes que aparezcan en la escena lleven un traje de poesía y al mismo tiempo que se les vean los huesos, la sangre."

The rest of the Spanish is stolen from conversations with Ela. This poem was first published in the *Chicago Quarterly Review*.

"DETAIL : GARNET"
I lifted and modified Jericho Brown's "Duplex" form, in *The Tradition* (Port Townsend, WA: Copper Canyon Press, 2019).

"SEASIDE GRAFFITI"
I can't say how many of my friends died or fell off the face of the planet after the pharma companies changed the formulation of Oxycontin so you couldn't rail it anymore. Once that happened, people switched to heroin because it was cheaper. I think we were sixteen? Ronny died when I was in grad school at the University of East Anglia finishing my MFA. This poem was published in the *White Review* in the UK in 2010.

When I was editing these pieces for this project, my best friend Steve Cafagna OD'd and died. His girlfriend called my phone at 2 am on June 16, 2019, and texted me after she called the ambulance: "Its desiree. I have steves phone for awhile . . . We were together when his heart stopped. I tried to do the chest compressions until paramedics got there. I tried." I have that text still.

"CONCERNING THE FOX"
The *Liber Monstrorum* (*Book of Monsters*) is a late seventh- or early eighth-century Latin catalogue of monsters, half-men, serpents, and fabulous races of people.

Ladrón de Manzanas: literally, Apple Thief. This is a hard cider in Spain with an image of a fox on it.

Crux interpretum: a hard passage to interpret; a passage that acts as a crossroads for the meaning of a piece.

Spanish is mostly stolen from real or imagined conversations with

Ela and from ex votos on the walls around the Alhambra.

This poem was first published in the *Chicago Quarterly Review*.

"DETAIL : LIBER MONSTRORUM"
"You have asked about the secret arrangement [or 'filthiness'] of
the lands of the earth, and if as many kinds of monsters are to be
credited as are demonstrated in the hidden parts [or 'births'] of the
world. . . ," from the prologue of *Liber Monstrorum*, translated by
Andy Orchard.

Andy Orchard, *Liber Monstrorum: A Translation of the Old
English Text by Andy Orchard* (January 18, 2005). https://web.
archive.org/web/20050118082548/http://members.shaw.ca/
sylviavolk/Beowulf3.htm.

"FLORILEGIUM : VOYNICH MANUSCRIPT"
"But I say unto you, That whosoever is angry with his brother without
a cause shall be in danger of the judgment: and whosoever shall say
to his brother, Raca, shall be in danger of the council: but whosoever
shall say, Thou fool, shall be in danger of hell fire." Matthew 5:22 KJV

King James Bible, (Oxford University Press, 2008; originally
published 1769).

"But what if I should discover . . . that the very fiend himself is
within me and that I myself stand in need of the arms of my own
kindness? That I myself am the enemy that must be loved, what
then? Then as a rule, the whole truth of Christianity is reversed.
There is then no more talk of love and long suffering. We say to the
brother within us *raca* and we condemn and rage against ourselves.
We hide him from the world. We deny ever having met this least
among the lowly in ourselves and had it been God himself that
drew near to us in this despicable form, we should have denied him
a thousand times before a single cock had crowed."—Alan Watts
(1960) reading a lecture by Carl Jung to Swedish clergymen deliv-
ered in the 1930s. I accessed the Alan Watts reading in 2017.

I live in southern California. Our state burns hotter and hotter every year. This poem was first published in *The Adirondack Review* as "Fire Season" in 2016.

"ADAM & ADAM"

"Adam & Adam" is a blended expansion from "The Song of an Embarrassed Man" (1913) by Velimir Khlebnikov and "Businessman from Mongolia. Irkutsk" by Amarsana Ulzytuev (2019), first published in translation in *Words without Borders*, April 2017 edition, translated by Alexander Cigale and published in Russian in 2019 in *Arion*:

> Как ворон на голой ветке, на крыше высотки сидит одиноко,
> Вконец обанкротившийся, с высоты 13-го этажа, свесил
> ноги. (2019)

Like a raven on a stripped branch, sitting alone on the roof of
  a highrise.
Having lost everything, from the height of the thirteenth floor,
  dangles his feet. (2017)

How strange; as a skeleton
I come to you in the evening
And, holding out my long hand,
Fill the living room with constellations. (1913)

"BEN'S RANCH : A FENCE OF CLOUDS"
This poem was first published in *The Chestnut Review* in 2021.

"*ANSIA* : REACH"
The Spanish is stolen from real or imagined conversations with Ela.

λέγω • (légō): I call, name (usually in the passive voice).

"Language disguises the thought; so that from the external form of the clothes one cannot infer the form of the thought they clothe, because the external form of the clothes is constructed with quite another object than to let the form of the body be recognized."

Ludwig Wittgenstein, *Tractatus Logico-Philosophicus* (Routledge & Kegan Paul, 1922).

"The phenomenological world is not the bringing to explicit expression of a pre-existing being, but the laying down of being. Philosophy is not the reflection of a pre-existing truth, but, like art, the act of bringing truth into being."

Maurice Merleau-Ponty, *Phenomenology of Perception* (Routledge & K. Paul; Humanities Press, 1974).

"DETAIL : λέγω"
The form of "Detail : λέγω" is lifted (unmodified) from Jericho Brown's "Duplex" form in *The Tradition* (Port Townsend, WA: Copper Canyon Press, 2019).

"WHITE ELEPHANTS"
"I'd do anything for you."
"Would you please please please please please please please stop talking?"
He did not say anything but looked at the bags against the wall of the station. There were labels on them from all the hotels where they had spent nights.
"But I don't want you to," he said, "I don't care anything about it."
"I'll scream," the girl said.

From "Hills Like White Elephants," Ernest Hemingway (1927).

"TONIC KEY : A ROSE"
"What must be admitted is that the definite images of traditional psychology form but the very smallest part of our minds as they actually live . . . Every definite image in the mind is steeped and

dyed in the free water that flows round it. With it goes the sense of its relations, near and remote, the dying echo of whence it came to us, the dawning sense of wither it is to lead. The significance, the value, of the images is all in this halo or penumbra that surrounds and escorts it,—or rather that is fused into one with it and has become bone of its bone and flesh of its flesh; leaving it, it is true, an image of the same thing it was before, but making it an image of that thing newly taken and freshly understood."

William James, *The Principles of Psychology* (Holt, 1890).

"You can't step in the same river twice."

Heraclitus

"For I am the one who brings into being for myself—and thus into being in the only sense that the word could have for me—this tradition that I chose to take up or this horizon whose distance from me would collapse were I not there to sustain it with my gaze (since this distance does not belong to the horizon as one of its properties)."

Maurice Merleau-Ponty, *Phenomenology of Perception* (Routledge & K. Paul; Humanities Press, 1974.)

"We don't recreate or copy the external stimuli we perceive, we constitute them, construct them and the foundation of that construction (apperception?) is our entire past and projected lives at the instant—we see the worlds we carry with us."—My notes from the margin.

"Language is a conspiracy between two people."

—Sadhguru

"ONE"

"I am black, and comely, O ye daughters of Jerusalem, as the tents of Kedar, as the curtains of Solomon."

Song of Solomon 1:5

King James Bible (Oxford University Press, 2008; original work
  published 1769).

"DETAIL : HELIOTROPE"
Do pronouns really matter? Cutter Streeby : we/us/ours

"FRAMEWORK : I"
"A mood 'comes neither from "outside" nor from "inside," but arises
out of Being-in-the-world, as a way of such being' (*Being and Time,*
29: 176). Nevertheless, the idea that moods have a social character
does point us toward a striking implication of Heidegger's over-
all framework: with Being-in-the-world identified previously as a
kind of cultural co-embeddedness, it follows that the repertoire of
world-disclosing moods in which I might find myself will itself be
culturally conditioned."
  Michael Wheeler, "Martin Heidegger," *The Stanford
    Encyclopedia of Philosophy* (Fall 2020 edition), Edward N.
    Zalta, ed., https://plato.stanford.edu/archives/fall2020/
    entries/heidegger/.

ABOUT THE CONTRIBUTORS

MICHAEL HAIGHT (b. 1984) was raised in the towns of Perris and Hemet, California. He received a BA in Creative Writing from the University of California–Riverside, and an MFA in Visual Art from Claremont Graduate University in Claremont, California. The major themes of Haight's practice include the paths and failures of enlightenment, and the creation and return of karmic energy. The artist has exhibited in solo and group exhibitions in Los Angeles, New York, and Seoul.

CUTTER STREEBY holds a MFA from the University of East Anglia and an MA in Literature from King's College, London. He has delivered many lectures on poetics, translation, and translation theory, including "Navigating Lese Majeste: Translating the Poetry of Zakariya Amataya," at universities across Thailand and Malaysia while teaching at the graduate and undergraduate levels. Publications, translations, and anthologies include *The White Review, Anthology of South East Asian Poets* (Vagabond Press), *Chicago Quarterly Review, Chestnut Review, Hayden's Ferry Review, Cincinnati Review,* and *World Literature Today,* among others. He successfully exited his first marketing startup, GraylingAgency.com, in 2020.